BLOCKCHAIN

How to Safely Create Stable and Long Term Passive Income by Investing in Bitcoin

Table of Contents

Introduction 1

Chapter 1: How to Determine if Bitcoin Is the Right Investment for You.. 3

Chapter 2: Finding the Right Wallet and Exchange 17

Chapter 3: Familiarizing with Proven Investment & Trading Strategies for Bitcoin... 41

Chapter 4: Being Aware of the Risks 65

Chapter 5: Diversifying Your Digital Currency Investments 75

Conclusion 83

INTRODUCTION

You're about to discover how to safely invest in Bitcoin, potentially earning you a secondary income in the most passive way possible.

Filled with current information and practical guidance, this book will show you how to:

- Determine if Bitcoin and other digital currencies are good investment vehicles for you.
- Look for the right exchange for trading Bitcoin.
- Learn the most effective strategies in Bitcoin investing.
- Be familiar with the risks of investing in digital currencies.

Digital currencies such as Bitcoin are regarded as the money of the future, and there is a high potential anyone to make substantial profits if they decide to ride with this trend early on. But there are risks to avoid and strategies to follow if you want your investment to be successful.

It's time to find out more.

CHAPTER 1

HOW TO DETERMINE IF BITCOIN IS THE RIGHT INVESTMENT FOR YOU

Before we discuss the factors that will guide you in your decision to invest or trade in Bitcoin, you need first to understand the difference between investing and trading. Even if you assume that you already know the difference, I still encourage you to review this basic knowledge so you will be refreshed and probably learn more.

Basically, investing and trading are two distinct strategies of trying to make a profit in the financial world. The primary purpose of investing is to grow wealth over an extended period of time by purchasing and holding a portfolio of stocks, bonds, funds, and other financial instruments.

Investors usually increase their profits via compounding or through the process of reinvesting the profits and dividends into added shares of stock. The investments are usually held for a certain period of time, which could range in weeks, months, years, or even decades. Investors could also take advantage of the perks involved in investments such as dividends and interest.

Although just like other markets, Bitcoin's price fluctuates, investors can still ride out the risk with the projection that the price will soon recover and any loss will gradually be restored. Investors usually refer to market fundamentals in looking for investments such as management forecasts and price/earnings ratios.

On the other hand, trading involves higher frequency of buying and selling financial instruments such as commodities, stocks, or currency pairs. The primary objective of trading is to generate profits that can outperform investments. An active trader may be aiming for a 10% monthly profit compared to the 10% possible profit of an investor. The profits in trading are generally made by buying instruments at a lower rate than selling them at a higher price within a shorter term. Conversely, you can also make profits by selling when the price is higher and then buying to cover when the price is lower. This is also called as the selling short in order to still make profits despite of the falling trend in the market.

While investors are normally trained in waiting out for less profitable positions, traders are accustomed to take losses or profits within a particular period of time. Protective stop loss orders are often used by traders to immediately deal with losing positions at a pre-determined price. Traders are also trained in using tools for technical analysis such as stochastic oscillators and moving averages in order to look for the trading setups with high potential to yield profits.

In Bitcoin exchange, you can make profits through investing or trading cryptocurrencies. Investors are looking for higher returns over a particular period through buying and then holding the Bitcoin. On the other hand, Bitcoin traders usually take advantage of the rising and falling markets to take more regular profits.

Now that you have hopefully learned the difference between trading and investing, let us explore the different factors that can help you decide whether

Bitcoin could be the best investment or trading instrument for you.

Why Invest or Trade Bitcoins?

Trading or investing in Bitcoin can be a valuable endeavor regardless of your experience in the financial markets. The instrument is fairly new, still fragmented and currently had wide spreads. Margin trading and arbitrage are also now very common, so most people can still make profits in trading or investing in Bitcoins.

The record of volatility and bubble of Bitcoin has probably done more to entice more investors or traders than any other aspects of cryptocurrency. Every expected Bitcoin "bubble" just creates hype for this cryptocurrency, which makes it very popular. The publicity causes its price to increase because more and more investors and traders become interested.

Because to the uninformed, Bitcoin may seem a digital gold rush - a modern-day venture that you can do anywhere you want as long as you have your computer. However, the reality is this: many traders and investors give up after only several months or when they experience a market crash. They failed to understand that this is the nature of Bitcoin as a financial instrument. It has high volatility and the price can fluctuate extremely in only a matter of hours.

This doesn't mean you should close this book and forget about owning a percentage of what is highly regarded as the future currency. The point here is that you need first to understand the nature of Bitcoin - its similarities to traditional financial instruments and its uniqueness as a cryptocurrency.

When Bitcoin was developed during the early 2008, it was phenomenal because it is first of its kind, unlike any other currency in the world. But today, Bitcoin is only one, although yes the most popular, of the hundreds of cryptocurrencies that are all using cryptography to regulate the production and value transfer.

In spite of the name, there is no actual coin, because Bitcoin is a purely digital currency that is transferred directly from one peer to another.

Among the best advantages of Bitcoin is its decentralized system. There is no need for a third-party in the middle or a central entity to manage the transfer. Hence, it is possible to send money to anyone regardless of their location or time zone, which eliminates the need for conventional organizations such as banks or wire transfer companies. Also, the system eliminates the need to pay extraordinary fees or wait for several days for the money to appear at your bank account. You can send and receive Bitcoins in as fast as a few minutes.

All Bitcoin transactions that have ever occurred are logged in a public ledger, which is based on the blockchain technology. This ledger allows any member of the Bitcoin network to access the ledger and review the history of transactions. Hence, it can be extremely difficult to defraud the system. If there is any dubious transaction, the whole network will know.

Despite of its benefits, there is still no way to be certain if Bitcoin or other similar digital currencies will eventually entirely replace the common currencies that we use today. But it is clear that it has sparked a revolution that the world will eventually learn how to use. After all, money was an innovation thousands of years ago, and it has become widespread.

What Is So Unique about Bitcoin?

Bitcoin is special and one-of-a-kind because of the technology that supports it and the innovative idea of being free from any controlling organization. However, before you start investing or trading Bitcoin, there are several things that you need to understand about the nature of this cryptocurrency.

Bitcoin Can Be Used Worldwide

Bitcoin is not a common currency, so its price is not directly affected by the economy or policies of one government or state. Bitcoin has had its share of roller-coaster ride before it became established, and most of them are associated with global events.

For example, the sudden spike in Bitcoin prices in 2013 was related to the economic crisis in Cyprus. Because the government has frozen the money of its citizens in the bank, there was an increased interest in looking for other ways to spend and receive money other than conventional banks. Bitcoin was among the top alternatives during those times as many opted to reinvest their money and prevent further loss. Nevertheless, there is no one central authority or a person who can regulate Bitcoin.

You Can Trade / Invest in Bitcoin Anytime

Remember, there is no official platform for exchanging Bitcoin. Therefore, there is no official price for this cryptocurrency. Not similar to stock markets that have specific operating hours or closes during weekends, you can still buy or sell Bitcoin anytime even when it is in the wee hours or the night.

Most of the exchanges are in the same range of price, but there are also some opportunities for arbitrage. Meanwhile, Bitcoin can really surprise you with its fluctuations.

Bitcoin Has High Volatility

Bitcoin became popular because of its frequent and fast price fluctuations, which is quite often within a day. This is actually a major disadvantage for investors, but an enticing opportunity for traders to make high profits fast.

Trading Vs. Investing Bitcoin

There is a significant difference between trading and investing in Bitcoin - just like in other traditional financial instruments - investing money on cash is quite different when you trade on stocks. But when it comes to Bitcoin, you need to learn about buying cryptocurrency.

It can be very easy to buy Bitcoin - depending on the different exchanges and wallets. However, this is nothing like buying foreign currency when you are in a foreign soil. It is actually not rocket science. You just need to look for the right exchange, wallet and pay for the coins.

Hence, buying Bitcoin is common among people who just want to try the currency and invest some of it, or for those who are just curious about this new commodity.

On the other hand, investing is a long-term strategy working on a portfolio containing various cryptocurrencies, traditional risk hedging, and business insights. More often than not, Bitcoin investors are not focusing that much on the volatility of Bitcoins and not that keen on giving up the investment immediately when price fluctuates.

Trading Bitcoins is usually a part of a short-term strategy. You can try the market, observe how to trade for a few weeks or months, and sell the commodity as soon as you think that the price is at its peak. Therefore, Bitcoin traders are very sensitive to price fluctuations and can easily give up the trade once it becomes unprofitable.

The Risks of Trading Bitcoins

Even though there are risks associated with both investing and trading Bitcoins, the latter carries much more vulnerability because of the dynamic nature of this cryptocurrency. Investors are more willing to survive the crash and they usually have the backup resources so they can sustain the effects of a market downturn. On the other hand, traders are usually compared to gamblers, because they need to respond to the market conditions fast and they are skilled in determining if it is the right time to call the game. Most risks in trading Bitcoin are usually associated to the mistakes of inexperienced traders such as leaving their currencies on one exchange.

Many of the cryptocurrency exchanges have their preferred wallets where you can store Bitcoins, which can make the trading easier. But of course, it is not the most secured way. For example, one of the most popular demise in the history of Bitcoin is the meltdown of Mt. Gox, which is a Japanese exchange for Bitcoin. During its heyday, it was the biggest exchange for cryptocurrencies, especially Bitcoin. It was popular as an easy to use platform for buying cryptocurrencies. But this system collapsed, and resulted in the loss of more than 800,000 BTC, which was never retrieved and refunded to the customers.

As an assumption, if you are considering Bitcoin trading, you also have substantial money that you can place on the market. You should be careful and invest only in reliable and secure wallet. Remember that no one is regulating the exchange so it can be busted anytime as well as your money. Despite of a new platform for trading or investing, the classic rule still applies - never put all your eggs in one basket.

Capital Risk in Bitcoin Trading

If you want to try Bitcoin, there is a high chance that you have experienced investing or trading with traditional money first. Of course, you will never begin with all of your capital, as you need first to experience and properly understand the market first.

This is also true with trading Bitcoin. However, many beginners are usually disillusioned with the idea of how much they could make from Bitcoin trading. This is certainly a more vibrant exchange and the rates are moving faster compared to a conventional stock exchange. But this also carries a higher risk. The movements on the value of a traditional currency could be measured in a small portion of a dollar. On the other hand, Bitcoin rates can rise and fall on extreme ends several times a day.

Should You Trade or Invest in Bitcoin?

There is no general answer for this question, because the most suitable option will depend on your knowledge in the platform as well as your available resources. You can start investing in Bitcoin from a small amount that can keep on growing as time passes by and as you acquire more experience. This is also a long-term strategy that could gradually lead to generating a huge amount of money. This can also ease up the high volatility of Bitcoin, as it will allow you to master the market and prevent losing your investments.

On the other hand, trading is often ideal for those who are more adept in the nature and depth of the cryptocurrency and those who are brave. The regular fluctuation of Bitcoin prices could be a tremendous experience for any trader, but it could also scare away those who don't have any experience.

CHAPTER 2

FINDING THE RIGHT WALLET AND EXCHANGE

Buying Bitcoin is an important skill to make profit in digital currency trading or investing. It is crucial to know which Bitcoin exchange to choose. Because you have to invest your money into the Bitcoin and the exchange from where you can purchase them, it is important to make sure that you are selecting the right one.

In this Chapter, we will discuss the ideal exchange to choose from depending on your investment or trading objective. Take note that these are only recommendations to help you decide which platform to choose. Matters will always change according to the exchange and the digital currency market. Hence, it is crucial to do your due diligence first.

Your Location

It is important that you know where the exchange is based in your country, because the laws and regulations that govern trading and investing in digital currencies may vary from one state to another. Purchasing Bitcoins in your home country is ideal. A simple Google search will allow you to find the list of exchange country locations.

Most exchanges are accepting different fiat currencies, so payment is not an issue. Just be sure to check the fine print. Read the terms of service especially the currencies that are accepting.

How to Pay for Bitcoins?

Almost all of Bitcoin exchanges are accepting payments via cash, wire transfers, bank transfers, credit cards, PayPal, and other forms of digital payments. You can choose what is convenient for you. Just make sure to consider your privacy as using credit card is the least private option, while paying with cash is the safest, although entails some level of effort in your part.

Transaction Fees

You need to ensure that the transaction fees charged by the exchange are reasonable and are not too high compared to other alternatives in the market. The fees may change overtime and may also vary from one exchange to another. There are some exchanges that are charging for added fees apart from the transaction or exchange fees.

Order Volume

One indicator of the stability and strength of an exchange is its order volume, which they will publish on their site. Basically, the order volume is just a list of orders that are currently offered by the exchange. Higher volume order indicates that more people are on the exchange and so it has high liquidity. Even though this is a vital factor to consider, you should take note that an exchange that does not publicize its order volume doesn't mean it is illegal. Chances are, the platform has not yet enabled the feature or has a lower volume.

Exchange Transparency

Transparent exchanges usually publish cold storage addresses and they normally audit information to easily confirm their Bitcoin reserves. Audits are standard practice for the exchange to show to its customers that they are liquid and can easily cover all sales. This also shows that they are not operating on a percentage exchange.

Fulfillment

Also consider the time that you can receive your Bitcoins after buying them. Be sure to also verify if the exchange is offering locked in prices, which means that the price you buy is the price you can be charged if the Bitcoins are taking several days to be credited to your wallet.

Privacy

Keeping your transactions totally anonymous can be difficult in Bitcoin, unless you are purchasing locally from someone through cash through a P2P exchange. Be sure to verify if the exchange you are choosing has a standard Know Your Customer or KYC practice.

You may need to provide personal details before you can buy Bitcoins from these exchanges.

Security

It is crucial to know that the exchange is safe and secure. Check if the site is HTTP or HTTPS. A site that has a security protocol has HTTPS. Also check if the exchange offers secure log-ins alongside other security measures such as two-factor authentication. Security is a non-negotiable factor to consider in choosing your exchange to trade or invest Bitcoins.

Online Reputation

You can easily know the reputation of the exchange you are considering to choose by reviewing customer reviews and online feedback on online forums such as Reddit. It is safe to trust an exchange with a lot of positive reviews compared to an exchange with very minimal online presence.

Top Bitcoin Exchanges

Because of the popularity and the high promise of returns for Bitcoin trading or investing, there are now numerous Bitcoin exchanges that you can choose, each offering different terms and payment options. Below are the top exchanges you can use to buy your first Bitcoins. All these options are accepting US Dollars as well as other major currencies or other digital currencies.

Coinbase

Coinbase is among the most reliable exchange platform for Bitcoins today. It is popular for Bitcoin investors and traders because of its dollar cost averaging method, wherein users could choose to automate their purchase weekly or monthly. It is also known for its simplistic platform for buying and selling Bitcoin. It is also interesting to take note that this exchange is monitoring all transactions for dubious accounts and may even close accounts without prior notification.

LocalBitcoins

LocalBitcoins is described as more of a platform and less of an exchange where individual traders and investors from around the globe can connect with each other. You can choose to go to an area-specific page and you can choose who you would like to trade Bitcoins with. It also comes with an escrow system that protects the buyer and the seller until the transaction is complete. This is the best platform if you are looking for direct trading, but you should exercise caution since there are also reports of scammers lurking in the exchange, some of which are using stolen information and fake bank transactions.

BitQuick

As the name implies, BitQuick offers fast transactions. The platform operates like the LocalBitcoin, because you can also buy and sell Bitcoins directly from individuals. Buying Bitcoins using BitQuick costs 2% of the fee, while selling is free. You can use this exchange if you are looking for speedy transactions, and you shop around if speed is not that important for you.

BitStamp

BitStamp is now five years and the first exchange to be licensed operator by Bitcoin. It is a preferred exchange because of the platform's ability to process payments using credit cards. There is also an option to withdraw Bitcoins as actual gold, which is a unique selling point of this exchange. Choose this platform if you are searching for a reliable Bitcoin exchange. Also take note that the company is monitoring transactions for dubious activities and will close suspicious accounts without prior notice.

Kraken

Kraken is an exchange that specializes in trading Bitcoins that has an outstanding reputation in the financial markets, and is actually one of the first exchanges to pass audit from an independent firm. Make sure that when you use this exchange, you know how to setup the two-factor authentication as there were reports of accounts being drained when users ignored this security feature.

BTC-e

BTC-e is known for its transparent transactions. It is possible to see a live tracker with the prevailing Bitcoin rate as well as the most recent transactions in the platform from the trade's history. It also comes with a chatbox, where users can talk with each other. This unique feature will allow you to learn from industry insights as well as the current sentiments of Bitcoin traders and investors.

OK Coin

OK Coin is a Bitcoin exchange company that is popular among traders and investors. It is a non-winner when it comes to the aesthetics of the platform, but it is known for its practical features. This is recommended for traders with enough experience and decent expertise in using the tools and platform for Bitcoin trading.

ItBit

ItBit is a trading platform where you can buy and sell Bitcoins. This exchange provides reasonable prices for Bitcoins, but take note that there is a minimal fee. This exchange is also known for offering boutique service for trades that are more than 100BTC. However, this exchange may not be the best platform for you if you are looking for small Bitcoin trades.

Circle

Circle is a visually-stunning Bitcoin exchange and ideal for casual Bitcoin users. This is promoted as a user-friendly payment channel that comes with chat function. You can also link your credit card or debit card so you can send money to your family and friends through blockchain. Use this channel if you are only looking for funds transfer solution instead of investing in Bitcoin for long-term.

E-Coin

This Bitcoin exchange platform is popular among those who buy Bitcoins using their debit cards. I have also included this in our list because the exchange allow you to purchase Bitcoin through PayPal, which is actually rare. While you can also purchase Bitcoins using PayPal through VirWox or Paxful, they carry higher charges.

Choosing a Bitcoin Wallet to Keep Your Digital Currency

After choosing the most suitable exchange for you, the next step is to find a Bitcoin wallet where you can keep your purchased digital currency. Because you are investing your money into Bitcoin, selecting the most appropriate wallet for you is an essential step, which you should not ignore. There are many available wallets today, which includes the official wallet of the Bitcoin network.

But before choosing your wallet, we first need to discuss the factors that you must consider. The situation may change based on the market conditions and the stability of your chosen wallet. However, you will be more successful if you do your due diligence first.

Wallet Security

Ensuring that the wallet you choose is safe to use is crucial and must not be ignored. Take note that if you are using a web wallet, you must always be certain that the website is using a secure protocol or HTTPS. Also check if the wallet is using strong logins such as two-factor authentication.

Transparency

Is the Bitcoin wallet you choose transparent in who they are and how they operate? Also check if the site's code is open source. If not, it can be difficult to ensure that the wallet is really secure. Open source code could be independently checked for vulnerabilities. Also try to find out if the site's source code is updated.

User Experience

Try to determine if the wallet is easy to use or if it takes some effort. Ideally, you must choose a wallet that is simple and does not require too much fiddling before you get started. You should also consider how you will use your Bitcoin, too. Keep in mind that a wallet that is specifically designed and optimized for mobile devices can be ideal if you are usually mobile. If you consider yourself already advanced, you can try using a full Bitcoin client directly to your computer. There are also other options that may include hardware devices so you can also keep your Bitcoins even if you are not connected online.

Privacy

Is privacy crucial for your Bitcoin investments? Is there a need for you to register before you can use the wallet? Does your chosen exchange accept minimal registration details before you can use it? Does the site use user-verification process such as Know Your Customer (KYC)? These are among the most important things to take note before you make a final decision.

Multisignature

Aside from securing the wallet, also check if it offers a multisig option. This is an ideal option if you want your Bitcoin to be safe from online hackers. Multisignature refers to the requirement of more than one key access before you can use the site. This is like opening a box that requires two people with two separate keys to open the box.

HD Wallets

Try to find digital wallets that are already HD or Hierarchical Deterministic, which use new Bitcoin addresses that increase user privacy. Privacy is an important concern in Bitcoin investing, and HD wallets carry advanced security features because of their well-rounded infrastructure.

Backup

Backing up your data is also an essential aspect of Bitcoin wallets. Does the digital wallet that you are considering offers a way to back up your data? Does the platform offers data encryption? Is there a backup restoration process and can you use it without too much effort? Try to explore these options before you load your purchased Bitcoins to your wallet.

Control

Technically, you don't have any control over your wallet if you don't have the access to the private keys. This is a vital factor to consider when you are selecting a Bitcoin wallet. You must have the ability to access your wallet so you have control over your purchased digital currency. This will allow you to move your wallet anytime, and backup your data.

Take note that Bitcoin transactions cannot be reversed. In order to send or spend Bitcoins, you should have the private and public keys. Protecting your private key is your responsibility as an investor or a trader.

Types of Wallets

There are several types of Bitcoin wallets and they offer different levels and processes for security to make sure that the private keys are protected. Basically, there are five categories of Bitcoin wallets: desktop, online, paper, mobile, and hardware. Some categories may overlap or use hybrid solutions. We will discuss each category and the example of available wallets.

Desktop Wallet

Desktop wallets are regarded as the best type of wallets if you are looking for secured storage of Bitcoin. You need to download the software into your desktop PC or laptop and complete transactions using the software, which may not be practical for people who are always on the go. It can also be confusing for beginners in Bitcoin Investing. Below are the top examples of desktop wallets:

Bitcoin Core

This Bitcoin wallet is regarded as the first and original digital currency wallet. It provides you control over your private and public keys that guarantees safe storage. The major downside is that the software requires substantial disk space because it carries the data on each transaction you perform. You have to allocate at least 65GB of free space before you can download the wallet, and you must take note that this space requirement will increase over time as you perform Bitcoin transactions.

Multibit

Compared to Bitcoin Core, Multibit only requires 30MB for downloading. Most Bitcoin traders and investors are using this wallet together with Keep Key (you will learn more about this later), which is a flash drive that will request manual verification before a Bitcoin transaction could be completed.

Armory

Armory is a popular desktop wallet because it is regarded as the only open-source wallet with multi-signature support and cold storage. The private keys will be kept in an offline desktop, so only you will have access to the keys.

Online Wallets

Online Bitcoin wallets are wallets, which you can access via the Internet using any device as long as you can be connected online. These wallets are easier to use because of its accessibility. However, this is more vulnerable to attacks such as malware, phishing, and hacking. In fact, the meltdown of online wallets such as Bitfinex and Mt. Gox have made Bitcoin investors and traders wary of this category.

Even though the Bitcoin online wallets listed below are known for their reliability, it can be wiser to store larger amounts of Bitcoins in other categories of wallets.

BitGo

A trusted name in the digital currency world, BitGo is regarded as a leader when it comes to securing blockchain technology. This wallet is ideal for individuals and businesses who like fast transactions. More often than not, a Bitcoin transaction requires around three to six verifications that may take between 30 to 60 seconds. With its zero-verification feature, BitGo allows Bitcoin investors and traders to process fast and secure transactions.

Blockchain.info

This wallet is regarded as the most popular because around 8 million Bitcoin traders are using this platform to check and process their transactions. This is a winner when it comes to cross-platform capacity, multi-country support, and ease of use. Apart from online wallet, Blockchain.info can also be accessed via mobile app and on desktop.

GreenAddress

A lot of Bitcoin traders and investors have the habit of checking their Bitcoin wallets several times in a day to ensure that their money is still intact. Frequent logins, especially if performed in unsecured Internet connection will make the account vulnerable to phishing or malware attacks. GreenAddress offers a watch-only platform that can help you to monitor your Bitcoin balances without the need to login every time you want to check your account.

Paper Wallets

Paper Bitcoin wallets are generally safe against online attacks because the Bitcoins are stored offline. You can control your digital currency anytime as you also protect your private keys. The primary disadvantage of using paper wallets is the storage. Paper can be easily lost, torn, or fade. There is also no way to recover paper wallets, so the money could be lost forever if you don't remember the private keys. This is an important factor to consider if you want to use paper wallets.

BitAddress

BitAddress offers a no-nonsense service, which allows you to produce Bitcoin paper wallets within a matter of minutes.

BitcoinPaperWallet

Using this platform, you can print paper wallets that are tamper-resistant. This wallet is also popular among Bitcoin traders and investors who are advocating for cold storage. The website also provides additional safety tips and supplies needed by Bitcoin traders and investors.

Mobile Wallets

Mobile Bitcoin wallets are practical to use and quite accessible. Many Bitcoin investors and traders are just using extra layers of security to make sure that their investments will not be wiped out by malicious attacks. It is often recommended to store Bitcoins for trading, while keep your Bitcoin investments in more secured wallets.

Wirex

This mobile Bitcoin wallet offers both online and mobile wallet service. It is popular among Bitcoin investors and traders because it is safe and easy to use. You can use multi-sig and enable two-factor authentication for both the app and your login on the platform, which makes it extremely difficult for third-parties to access your account.

Mycelium

Mycelium is known as one of the safest and most popular wallets available for secure storage of Bitcoin on mobile. Often promoted as a bank-grade wallet, Mycelium is categorized as an HD wallet with great features such as watch only mode and deletion of private keys.

Xapo

Popular for its secured mobile vault, Xapo integrates multi-sig technology and cold storage to ensure that the Bitcoins are protected from malicious attacks. Its actual servers are located in the Alps and contained in reinforced concrete walls with steel blast doors.

Hardware Wallets

Hardware wallets are often used by Bitcoin investors to store their high quantity of Bitcoins. Most hardware wallets are portable and easy to use. They also come with plug and play features that provide users complete control of their Bitcoins.

Trezor

Trezor is a reliable name and receives a lot of positive feedback online. It is well praised for its simplicity and no-nonsense features. It also comes with extra layer of security to prevent malware attacks and phishing. Its major advantage is the ability to recover Bitcoins in case of loss or theft.

Keepkey

Among the biggest fear of a Bitcoin investor is to be attacked by unknown user that may try to wipe out all their Bitcoin investments. KeepKey helps in preventing this from happening. You need to use the KeepKey device to manually approve every outgoing BTC transaction. Your private keys can be stored in the device, which is also protected by PIN in case it was stolen.

Ledger Nano

This is regarded as the smallest yet the most cost-effective solution in Bitcoin storage. It is about the size of a USB with several variations, commonly the Ledger Nano and the Ledger Nano S. The latter can also contain Ether - another popular digital currency.

For beginners, all these new learnings might be overwhelming. And you might still have second thoughts because of several news about Bitcoin investors who lost all their money due to malware, hacks, phishing, or just because of human error.

I recommend keeping your Bitcoin investments in hardware wallets or paper wallets, and if you have the resources, dedicate a high-powered computer so you can accommodate the space requirements of Bitcoin Core. If you prefer keeping your Bitcoins in mobile or online wallets, you may choose to spread them around in reliable websites such as those that are listed in this chapter.

CHAPTER 3

FAMILIARIZING WITH PROVEN INVESTMENT & TRADING STRATEGIES FOR BITCOIN

Investing and trading Bitcoin has its own sets of rewards and risks. It is just natural for people to be reluctant in investing on it if they know little about cryptocurrencies, but it has definitively demonstrated a surge in median price over the past years and shows high potential for the future. Most investors are venture capitalists who are trying to monetize on their expert foresight.

Is Bitcoin a Profitable Investment?

Experts predict that Bitcoin is on the verge of its boom, and those who got in early will be rewarded with increasing profits, despite of the fact that it does not yet have the same value and convenience of conventional currency. But with the fast development of advanced technologies for mining and distribution of Bitcoin, it is safe to say that more people will be able to use the currency in the future.

Set a Trading or Investment Plan

Whether you are interested to trade or invest in Bitcoin, you must always know how you can plan to make money. Are your profit margins enough for your portfolio? Building a retirement fund with a cryptocurrency portfolio will yield different results than day trading. Because the price of Bitcoin may heavily fluctuate depending on the demand of the market, it is crucial that you set a clear goal with realistic and practical values so you can easily decide whether you want to stay in trading or investing and when do you want to exit. Therefore, having a plan is highly beneficial and must be the first step in your trading or investing plan.

Organizational Investors Are Making a lot of Money

According to the oil tycoon Daniel Masters, Bitcoin will surge its value by at least 3000% over the next years. Over the past five years, organizational investors made about 92% return from their initial $350 million round, which supports a positive trend. One potential barrier, which makes high-level investment trickier is that the amount of financial control that that markets are imposing in transferring huge amount of cash into Bitcoin. For instance, US investors must first look for companies that can offer them with similar management and services for cryptocurrencies under an exemption from Securities and Exchange Commission.

Prepare for Price Fluctuations

It is quite common for Bitcoin price to fluctuate every now and then, even several times in a day. It is ideal for investors or traders to determine the reasons behind the fluctuation. Remember, Bitcoin is an innovative currency, which only a few companies accept as payment. This makes conventional regulation policy inapplicable, and various countries have the discretion to not support the currency. For instance, Indonesia has sent a warning to its citizens that although Bitcoin is not illegal, the use of cryptocurrency to pay for goods may infringe upon a few financial and economic laws of the country. Bitcoin is also vulnerable to rumors and bad news, because the price is closely related to the demand, and any bad publicity may have an effect in Bitcoin's total value.

Bitcoin May Even Replace Fiat Currency

Even if Bitcoin becomes successful for only about 50% of its prediction, the way we pay for goods and services will significantly change. Even though many investors believe that the ideal strategy is careful adoption, there are few features that Bitcoin has that could be more enticing compared to conventional currency. Basically, keeping digital currency will curtail the fees and regulations applied to conventional currency. In addition, the nature of the Bitcoin makes instant transactions, which allow for considerable reduction of delays on cash flows. Also, the transaction is virtual so security issues will be a primary concern. While conventional banks can monitor and immediately cancel credit cards that have been used in fraud, there is no single entity to manage the funds of an individual who fails to secure his or her personal keys.

Bitcoin Adds Novelty Value

Among the best ways to take Bitcoin and convert it into something that can offer extra value for your business is to accept Bitcoin. Because it is regarded as somewhat of a novelty, businesses like the New York City Bar EVR attracted a lot of publicity for being the first bar in New York City to accept Bitcoin payments.

As more services and industries start to acknowledge Bitcoins as a reliable and tradeable currency, the price will stabilize and increase in value. Investing into companies that are taking a risk is also a risk, but the reward can be very high.

You Can Mine Bitcoin

You can have access to Bitcoins if you choose to start your mining efforts. The primary factor to consider is the electricity cost as well as the initial equipment you need to buy. Because there are a range of equipment available in mining Bitcoins, it is possible to generate a huge income with a decent investment amount. There are also several organizations that are starting to mine Bitcoins, and even though most of them are not yet listed publicly, those who are deciding to invest in Bitcoin normally see an increase in stock prices. If you want to get serious about Bitcoin mining, the best strategy is to look for a location where maintenance costs can be minimal like locations with renewable and sustainable energy.

Strategies in Investing and Trading Bitcoins

Probably the best way to get involved in Bitcoin trading for profit is through an exchanger. You just need to join a P2P exchange marketplace such as LocalBitcoins or Bitsquare. Then, you can offer a service in your local area to buy and sell coins. In order to make some profit, you have to add a spread. For instance, you can offer to purchase 2% below the market price or sell 2% above. If you could offer comfortable ways for people to deal with you - possible even including personalized deals - and if you are always available to provide the service, then your customers will be happy to pay the spread.

However, you must be aware that you possibly need to make some deals by responding to other people's ads before you pay the spread yourself so you can gain reputation before you become known in your area and earn the trust of your customers.

There is no need for comprehensive financial analysis if you want to become an exchange, and this is the reason why this is arguably the best way to start in Bitcoin investing or trading. Being an investor or a day trader requires more skill and knowledge. Traders usually use online exchanges, and will target to buy or sell depending on whether they are projecting that the price will rise or fall. Traders may also provide a service, by filling out the order books with offers, which could be taken up by people who want to buy and sell for more practical purposes. However, the primary focus is not only on offering a service to customers, but nurturing relationships and providing great customer service. The focus is simply on making or taking offers, as a form of bet on whether the Bitcoin price will rise or fall.

As long as the market is not fluctuating too fast, you can still make profits as an exchanger regardless whether the price is rising or falling. But also, if the market is rising then it is ideal to purchase more than sell, by providing a better buy price and average selling price, or concentrating on buying. Hence, as an exchanger, you can increase your profits by becoming a trader, while providing exchange services will provide traders a safer way to experiment and test out your skills.

Even on a centralized platform, where you don't directly deal with the other person, you can still increase your profits by providing exchange services - by making offers instead of taking them. When you place offers into the order books instead of accepting offers that are already there, you can possibly gain a better price. Since you are also offering a service - you become the market maker that allows the exchange website to act as an exchanger without the need to accumulate huge amounts of your own capital by integrating your own liquidity. There are also exchanges who are offering incentives when you are making offers instead of taking them. These incentives may come in the form of lower trading fees, or even Bitcoin rewards and bonuses. Being an exchanger or a market maker as well as simply betting on the market rising or falling is a basic lesson that you can learn.

In order to become successful, you need to have a well-established strategy. You have to know precisely what you like when you are opening a trade - your target profit before you build up before taking it, how much loss you could stand before you give up and more. You have to know what time frame you are working on and what type of changes will make you review your strategy.

Following the Trend

Many financial markets will have long-term price rates, in which the whole movement will be in a single direction for several months or years at a time. A clear trend will stay even if the price will fluctuate several times a week or even days. Long-term traders and investors will usually look for this long-term trend and will place their investments in this direction. There is actually no need for you to identify the point at which a trend will turn and a new one starts in the opposing direction, as long as you don't need to cash out your investments soon. It will not matter if it takes you three to six months to confirm a new trend if an average trend takes a year to complete.

Fundamental Analysis

Stock market investors are familiar with fundamental analysis, which you can also use when trading

Bitcoins. This analysis requires you to look at the fundamental data that may affect the price of the cryptocurrency - such as the volume reported by businesses who are accepting Bitcoins, the volume traded on exchanges, number of daily transaction, number of wallet, number of active wallets, and many more. Then, you can use this data to project what you think is the actual worth of Bitcoin now. Your decision will depend on whether you think the Bitcoin is overvalued or undervalued and then sell or buy based on your assumptions.

While fundamental analysis is a common tool for investors to evaluate the various asset classes such as fiat currencies and equities, some analysts believe that using this strategy to assess Bitcoin can be more complicated.

For example, you may evaluate the stock of a company by simply looking at particular items on the balance sheet. But in the case of Bitcoin, there is no revenue or earnings that you can evaluate.

Hence, it can be difficult to derive an even remotely accurate valuation for Bitcoin if you depend on future cash flows the way you can evaluate other assets such as Apple stocks. As a response, traders and investors who are interested in performing fundamental analysis on Bitcoin have developed some new set of metrics.

Although Bitcoin has been regarded as a new form of asset class, the same rules can be used to fiat currencies. In addition, all the economic laws and theories also apply in full for digital currencies. So the beginning point for all fundamental analysis must be the supply and demand that can drive the prices.

The role of demand in evaluating Bitcoin

Several factors are affecting the demand of Bitcoin, which includes trading. Transaction activity, and adoption. Many analysts highlight the importance of user adoption that is critical to the long-term viability of digital currency. As for what is pushing the adoption of user, money can have different uses. Basically, money is used to store value, a unit of account, and a way of exchange. Beyond special groups, Bitcoin has never actually been used as a unit of account.

However, Bitcoin has managed to attract considerable traction as a medium of exchange. Hundreds of companies such as PayPal and eBay have agreed to accept Bitcoin since its launch in 2009.

On top of that, the number of daily verified transactions have generally followed a stable, upward trend based on a data released from Blockchain. The surge in transactions started in 2012 with more than 7,000 daily transactions recorded in April 2012, to an average of 30,000 transactions today.

But even though this data is considered as informative, this may not be the best factor to consider because there are still a large percentage of blockchain transactions that are generated by automated systems and do not actually signify economic activity. Rather, investors and traders should determine which transactions are made by actual people who are sending or receiving Bitcoins from another user.

As Bitcoin gains more popular adoption, there is a significant shift in concentrating on the digital currency as a platform of exchange and storage of value. The perception of Bitcoin as a way to store value is a primary driver of Bitcoin's price.

The Role of Supply in Evaluating Bitcoin

While Bitcoin demand may require complicated study, supply is a bit more direct. The blockchain protocol restricts the total number of Bitcoins at 21 million, and as of this writing, there are about 16.3 million Bitcoins that are in circulation. Moreover, the Bitcoin protocol also determines the rate of new supply. This sharply contrasts with the conventional currency model wherein the central bank has the ability to print money as it deems necessary. But there are also some limitations that are affecting the supply of Bitcoin.

Satoshi Nakamoto, the name used by the creators of Bitcoin is believed to own around 1.1 million BTC, which have not been accessed since they were mined. Most people in the community think they will not be used at all and even refer to this volume as dead BTC. Moreover, it is also impossible to determine how many dead BTC there are.

This is because during the early days of Bitcoin, the units have very low value. When the price started to increase, stories of people who have actually threw away their hard drives holding their private keys were very common.

Monitor the News

Similar to stock and forex, the price of Bitcoin will rise or fall depending on what is happening in the news. For instance, a major currency exchange attacked by malware, or a government announcing a strict policy on cryptocurrency will affect the price of Bitcoin, while unicorn companies getting funded through BTC or more liberal policies that support financial technology can influence the price to go up.

However, monitoring the news for Bitcoin investing or trading is not an ideal primary strategy, because you may not have the time to always hear the news first and respond promptly. More often than not, the market already will have reacted before you even learn the full story - even though if you have the time and the passion to hear the news, you might be able to use this in your investment arsenal.

Another strategy is to capitalize on correction. Usually, the market has the tendency to overreact to news, and as such, inexperienced traders or investors follow the trend without even analyzing the report. Hence, a 20% downturn, for instance, is usually followed by an increase between 5% and 10% as the market is correcting the overreaction. This will provide you an additional way to use news reports in Bitcoin investments.

Bitcoin Swing Trading

The strategies that we have discussed so far are considered as long-term or medium-term methods, because they may take months or years before they provide you great return, and you could easily end up with only minimal profits or even lose your investment. A faster way to make money with Bitcoin is through day trading, which is the method of buying and selling on the basis of short-term price fluctuations, over the course of days instead of months or years.

The most popular strategy for day trading is swing trading, which is a method that you can use to determine the turning points in short-term trends.

You can yield profits from the daily swings rise and fall in the BTC price, regardless of whether the long-term direction is rising or falling. This usually involves looking for resistance and support levels. The latter refers to the downward price level that is expected to meet resistance as buyers are coming into the market to buy a bargain. On the other hand, a resistance level refers to the scenario where a rising price move is expected to meet the resistance of sellers who are taking a profit.

Technical Analysis for Bitcoin

Technical analysis refers to the use of mathematical formula and chart patterns to project the future direction of price movement. Not similar to fundamental analysis, technical analysis is completely based on previous price data and possibly volume data. Hence, it says nothing about whether the price is too low or too high. Instead, technical analysts believe that there are specific repeating trends and patterns that will appear in any market.

Most of these are postulated to be based on human psychology, based on the theory that people will just tend to act in a specific way to different movements in the prices. Some investors also suggest that the changes in the actual value are influenced by the participants, and so studying these actions will provide you all the information you need to make a sound investment.

Users of technical analysis, also known as technicians or chartists are taking a practical approach by evaluating the history of the asset via price charts and using different analytical tools to understand how the market is feeling about Bitcoin.

While fundamental analysis is more on determining the worth of a security, technical analysis are more on monitoring the actual movement of the price. In looking at the price history of Bitcoin, you can try to identify common patterns such as resistance and support.

To better understand technical analysis, it is crucial to be familiar with the basic concepts of Dow Theory that has established the foundation for the practical strategy of analyzing securities.

Below are the basic assumptions of Dow Theory:

1. The movement in price is not totally random. Rather, they are following trends that can be either long-term or short-term. When a security is forming a trend, it is more likely to follow this trend than go against it. In using technical analysis, you can identify Bitcoin trends and make some profit from the price difference when you choose to buy or sell.

2. History repeats itself. You can predict the market via psychology, and you can respond in a similar manner when you are provided with the same stimuli. For instance, cryptocurrencies have regularly provided bullish responses to significant events such as news supporting the trend of wider adoption or higher visibility.

3. The market will discount everything. Remember, all previous, present, and even future information are already considered in the current price of an asset. For Bitcoin, this involves previous, present, and future demand on top of current regulations that are

affecting cryptocurrencies. The present price reflects all current information, which also involves the knowledge as well as expectations of all market participants. Hence, you can choose to understand what the price is saying about the market mood so you can make your smart predictions about the movement of the prices.

4. "What" is more important than "why". Chartists concentrate more on the price history of a security compared to the particular factors that have caused the movement of the price. Although any number of factors could have led to the movement of the security's price in a particular manner, chartists usually take a more straightforward approach by evaluating the current demand and supply.

Evaluating Trends

Evaluating the trends or the general movement of the security can help Bitcoin investors and traders. But, it can be a challenge to single out these trends. Cryptocurrencies are naturally very volatile, and evaluating a chart of the price movements of Bitcoin may likely reveal a sequence of rises and falls.

But through technical analysis, you can look past the volatility and determine the uptrend when you see a series of extreme rises and falls. In comparison, you can single out a falling trend when you pinpoint a series of highs and lower lows. Aside from this, you also need to factor in sideway trends wherein a security is experiencing little in the way of downward or upward trend.

You should understand that trends usually come in different lengths including long-term, mid-term, and short-term.

Moving Averages

One strategy that Bitcoin traders can use to easily spot trends is to look into the moving averages that can help in smoothing out the price fluctuations of a cryptocurrency so the Bitcoin traders and investors can better understand where the price is going.

The basic type of moving average is the simple moving average that is determined by computing the average price of a security over a certain period of time. For instance, you may look at what Bitcoin has done over a 10-day or 30--day period.

Another tool that you can use is the exponential moving average that can provide you better understanding of the recent price values when you are working on the average. When you analyze moving averages, you can get a better understanding of when the momentum may change. For instance, if a 5-day moving average falls under a 20-day moving average, this development will point to a bull market that is turning bearish. If the opposite takes place, with the shorter average rising above the longer average, the reverse is true.

The role of volume

You must bear in mind that volume plays a crucial role in assessing price trends. Low volume signifies weaker trends, while high volume indicates strong price trends. If the price of Bitcoin experience a significant gain or loss, you must be sure to assess the volume.

For instance, if the Bitcoin is experiencing a long uptrend and then sharply declines one day, you must check out the volume in order to gain a better understanding of whether this movement will represent a new trend or just a temporary setback.

In general, the rising of prices will coincide with the rising volume. If the price of Bitcoin experiences a rising trend, but the upward movement of Bitcoin take place in the middle of weak volume, this could mean that the trend is already running out of steam and may just fade away.

Bitcoin Trading Signals

The best thing about investing or trading nowadays is that you can always get the services of someone or a company to do it for you. These are known as signal providers who use technical analysis to provide you with the alerts when they think you must buy or sell Bitcoins. This works by paying a certain subscription fee and then you can get access to the trading signals.

Margin Trading

Margin trading is an ideal way to increase the fund you stand to make as profit or loss or from any fluctuation in the market. This is done by borrowing the funds you need to make the trade then using the

Bitcoins as collateral. For instance, you have $1000 to purchase Bitcoin. Rather than buying with this amount, you decided to borrow $9000 and buy $10,000 worth of BTC on a 1:10 leverage. If the price rises even by only 1%, you can gain 10%, but if the prices decreases only by 5%, you will lose 50% of the currency.

If you choose margin trading, you can also try automated systems that will allow you to sell if the market is moving too fast. This will limit your losses to less than the initial capital you have shelled out. Hence, in our example, if the price is dropping by 9%, then you will lose 90% of your funds. If this will continue, then you will lose all your investments including the money you owe. To put a stop to this, you can set a margin call, which will automatically close the investment for you.

Another way to make profit through margin trading Bitcoin is to use Electronically Traded Funds or ETFs, which are funds whose price tracks similar to Bitcoin. However, the fund doesn't really hold the coins. In general, this is only accessible and ideal for day traders, as all the trades will be closed at the end of the day. The main advantage is the lower fees compared to using major exchanges and you can also get instant access for 1:10 leverage, while the leverage that are usually available on the exchanges completely depends on what other investors are offering.

Bitcoin Futures

Futures refer to a contract that provides you the privilege to make a purchase at a certain price, at a certain date in the future. These could be used by people who are owning a lot of Bitcoins as a hedge, so that they will not lose as much if the price is going down. Speculators also use them as a way to make some profit by predicting if the value of the Bitcoin at a specific time will be higher or lower.

CHAPTER 4

BEING AWARE OF THE RISKS

Despite of the impressive returns and other potential benefits of Bitcoin, we can't deny the fact that this cryptocurrency, and its underlying technology is still on its very early stage. In general, no one is certain if it will be widely accepted or be seen as just a passing technological fad. The uncertainty that surrounds the future of Bitcoin is shown on its price volatility.

Whether you like to trade or invest in Bitcoins, there are several risks that you must be aware of:

Regulation

Possibly the largest risk to the future of Bitcoin as an investment vehicle and as a currency is the regulation of governments. For instance, if the United States decides to declare Bitcoin as an illegal currency, its price will definitely crash. US is one of the largest markets for Bitcoin investments, only next to China. Therefore, any critical regulatory changes will have a significant effect on the price and even the existence of the currency. The same goes for other starting hubs in Bitcoin such as Australia and the UK. If any world economy resists Bitcoin, the price will collapse and recovery may be a struggle.

Scalability

Another weak point of Bitcoin is the failure of the platform participants to agree on how to handle issues of scalability. In order for your Bitcoin investment to succeed, the blockchain has to be capable of handling higher volume of transaction compared to what it is processing now, and it should be able to do so within a shorter time frame. Today, the average Bitcoin transaction takes 30 minutes, which is just acceptable if you are wiring money abroad, but not that amazing when you are trying to pay for grocery. There are still few places where Bitcoins are accepted, which may likely to change. However, for now, the average person will usually purchase Bitcoin as investment.

The Bitcoin Core development team has already presented some great ideas on how to scale the cryptocurrency, and many of them are now lined up for testing and adapt it for the future. But the majority of Bitcoin miners who are supporting the blockchain should agree and be on board with the changes before their implementation. Without the agreement, the scalability of Bitcoin could be a challenge and may even lead to the cryptocurrency struggling as a currency for wider and broad transactions.

Wide-Scale Hacks on Bitcoin Exchanges

Another viable risk for Bitcoin is the potential wide-scale attacks on important Bitcoin companies as well as currency exchanges. The attack against Bitfinex in 2016 and Mt. Gox in 2014 have both significantly affected the price of Bitcoin.

According to research, since the introduction of Bitcoin in 2009, around 30% of Bitcoin exchanges have been hacked. In spite of the efforts to enhance cyber security at exchanges and Bitcoin companies, the risk of wide-scale hack is imminent and one that will most likely to happen again in the near future.

But high profile attacks must only have short-term effects on the Bitcoin price, and must not really affect its long-term price.

51 Percent Attack

Not all investors are aware of the 51 percent attack, which refers to a centralized Bitcoin mining operation taking more than half of the blockchain, at which point it can have the authority to reverse transactions that will make the whole blockchain unusable as no trust will be left in the platform. Currently, mining operations are happening around the world and the Bitcoin network is completely decentralized. But if one mining operation acquires a considerable amount of control over the blockchain beyond 50 percent, the future of Bitcoin as an acceptable global currency can be compromised.

Stronger Cryptocurrencies

Another disadvantage that is usually cited is that other stronger cryptocurrencies may overtake Bitcoin and may take its place as a primary investment vehicle. As we have discussed earlier, Bitcoin has some challenges such as scalability that could be improved or alleviated by a new digital currency, which can then go and dominate the platform. But it is true that Bitcoin has a first-mover advantage and the expansion of its ecosystem causes it to position so strong as the leading digital currency that this possibility may be very unlikely.

Moreover, research has revealed that the price of Bitcoin is more valuable compared to other emerging digital currencies, so for investors, holding Bitcoins may be better compared to betting on other cryptocurrencies trying to overtake its position.

Untraceable

Bitcoin is enticing for criminals because the transactions are untraceable. People may buy and sell drugs as well as other prohibited items with considerably less risk of being tracked by state authorities. In this regard, Bitcoins are comparable to regular cash that is used for crime or fraud. This feature may bring unwanted attention from state authorities that will ban Bitcoin.

Difficult to Trade

While there are many exchanges today that are offering services to buy and sell Bitcoins, it is not easy to transfer money to and from your PayPal account. However, this may likely to improve as more services will compete to provide easier solutions.

How to Reduce Your Risk Exposure when You are Trading or Investing in Bitcoin

Now that you understand the risks of trading or investing in Bitcoin, the next step is to learn effective ways so you can reduce your risk exposure.

Invest or Trade on Quality over Quantity

Traders or investors who are over trading the markets have the tendency to waste most money and time. Remember, the key to successful trading is to prioritize quality over quantity. Not every form of market condition will be ideal to your strategy. Automated scalping is more effective when the market is stable, while swing trading works best when the trends are strong. In order to find quality trades, you should first determine what trading style is best for you as well as going for the right market conditions.

Safeguard Your Investment from Counterparty Risk

Even though the digital currency markets offer the highest gains today, they still have their risks, and cryptocurrency exchanges come with a level of counterparty risk. Bear in mind that Bitcoin transactions are not reversible and trusting an exchange with your private pass could lead to substantial losses. As crypto traders or investors, you can't totally get rid of counterparty risk, but there are steps that you can do to significantly reduce the risks. This includes:

- Learn more about the exchange to ensure it has an outstanding reputation

- Diversify your Bitcoins across several exchanges

- Invest at least 70% to 80% of your portfolio, then trade the remaining percentage of your portfolio.

- Never leave your Bitcoins on an exchange if you are not actively trading

Avoid Using Too Much Leverage

Investors and traders normally use margins because they expand the order size, and this provides the flexibility of going short or long. As such, if you are using too much leverage, you may not have enough time to breathe and you could be at risk of losing your whole capital during the automated liquidation. Some exchanges are offering leverage as high as 100x, but with this, a simple 1% move can be devastating to your account. A more ideal approach is to use a 3x leverage, which will allow you to triple your gains while providing you enough buffer so you can immediately exit a bad trade. However, you may not do this if you are scalping time frames when the markets are too volatile. Basically, the longer you are holding the trade, the less leverage you have to use.

Stay Away from the Hype

Investors and traders have to deal with the fear of loss and missing out on good investment. By becoming a bit too greedy, you could end up purchasing tops.

Panic sell and you may just cash out too early. Emotional control and objectivity are key when you are investing in Bitcoin.

More often than not, when the hype is at its peak, the situation could be that the market will reach the distribution stage and a downtrend may follow. Mainstream media is usually late to the party, because they report on trends after the facts when the markets are over hyped. Be sure to get in before the herd then sell into your strength when the hype is already at its peak.

Plan Your Exit

Make sure that you identify the key support and resistance levels on your investment plan and map out your trades early on. Identify the risk to reward ratio and establish your targets for taking the profits. As an investor, you can add to your position when trends are strong or lock in your profits when you scale out along the way. In addition, you need to ensure to establish the stop orders to safeguard yourself when the markets move against you. Just take note that stops are not always effective when the price is moving too fast and you may experience some losses because of slippage.

CHAPTER 5

DIVERSIFYING YOUR DIGITAL CURRENCY INVESTMENTS

Diversification is a strategy that is commonplace among experienced investors. You can further diversify your investments in digital currency so you can maximize your return in different areas that will each respond differently to the same event. Even though this will not totally safeguard you against loss, diversification is one of the best strategies in any form of investing. While you can diversify your portfolio to include securities, fiat currencies, real estate, and other investment instruments, you can also choose to diversify your digital currency investments further by also considering other forms of cryptocurrencies other than Bitcoin that are showing great potential.

In this Chapter, you will get to know the top three digital currencies (Lite Coin, Ethereum, and Ripple) that are now playing in competition or in support role to Bitcoin.

Litecoin (LTC)

LiteCoin is another form of digital currency that also uses similar technology to Bitcoin. This was developed by Charlie Lee an ex-engineer at Google, who created this digital currency as an open-source payment channel that is also free from any restriction from a central authority. However, Litecoin is different from Bitcoin in areas such as using scrypt as a proof of work system and it offers faster block generation.

In essence, Litecoin is designed as a lower-scale digital currency of Bitcoin. Hence, if Bitcoin is gold, then Litecoin is considered as the silver. This was developed with the aim to resolve the flaws of the Bitcoin technology. Today, Litecoin also achieved peak volume and liquidity.

Production of Litecoin is faster compared to Bitcoin, particularly about 4x faster. Generally, Litecoin is now among the top digital currencies in terms of value. However, they are easier to acquire compared to most cryptocurrencies.

Like other digital currencies, Litecoin can also function as digital cash system. You can also use the Litecoin network to send or receive money. But instead of US dollars, it completes the transactions in Litecoins.

Also, Litecoin is also not issued by any single government. Instead of being controlled by a central bank and being printed or minted by the government, Litecoins are also produced through mining. This digital currency also uses a block where transactions are recorded. The block is also confirmed using a mining software and made accessible to any user who likes to see the block. When the miner confirms the transaction, the next block will be added to the chain.

The Litecoin network creates a block every 2.5 minutes, which is faster compared to the 10 minutes for Bitcoin.

Litecoin supply is also fixed currently at 84 million and the current conversion as of this writing is 1 LTC is equal to $47.31

Ethereum (ETH)

Ethereum is also a distributed public blockchain network. Even though there are some major technical differences between these two platforms, the most significant feature is that these two cryptocurrencies are substantially different when it comes to capacity and purpose.

Bitcoin provides one specific application of blockchain technology - a P2P digital currency system, which enables online payments. While the blockchain used in Bitcoin is used to monitor ownership of online cash, the blockchain used in Ethereum is used to run codes of any decentralized app.

In Bitcoin, you have to mine to earn coins. In Ethereum, you have to work in order to earn Ether, which can be seen as the fuel to the system. Currently, Ether is a tradeable cryptocurrency and can be used by app developers to pay for fees and services within the network.

Like most digital currencies, Ethereum is based on a P2P network, which any programmer can use to run Dapps or distributed applications. The network can run any computer program, but the network is designed to perform rules, which are executed if specific conditions are present similar to a contract. The Ethereum network uses its own public ledger to store, run, and secure these contracts.

Every computer on the network installs a small virtual machine that will sync with the blockchain and remains accessible to enforce contracts. The computer network easily provides the reliability, computing capacity, and security needed to perform the stipulated arrangements. Using the network is not free, so users only use it for consensus results.

Even though many examples of these contracts describe different human interactions, the platform is presently used for industrial use-scenarios such as communication between machines or stringent business logic between organizations. For example, there are power companies that are looking for ways to generate a smarter grid where residences can easily buy power. Another good example is the collaboration between Samsung and IBM for Internet of Things.

At present, the market cap of Ethereum is around $ 17 Billion, while the market capitalization of Bitcoin is at $ 34 Billion. Hence, Ether is regarded as the second most valuable digital currency today. This number is projected to rise in a span of a few more years.

Ripple (XRP)

Introduced in 2012, Ripple is a real-time worldwide settlement network, which provides affordable overseas payments. This digital currency allows banks to complete international payments in real-time at a fraction of a cost and transparency. With a market capitalization around $ 1.26 billion, Ripple is one of the most valuable digital currencies today.

Similar to Bitcoin and Litecoin, Ripple also maintains a blockchain known as a consensus ledger as its method of confirmation. However, it does not require mining so it decreases the need to use the computational power and also lessen network latency. The developers of Ripple believes that value distribution is a great way to incentivize specific behaviors and so they are now distributing the currency mainly via business development deals, offering XRP to organizational buyers who are interested to invest in the currency, and as rewards to providers of liquidity who provide tighter payment spreads.

Even though it was only introduced in 2012, Ripple was actually developed before Bitcoin. The project started in 2004 by Ryan Fugger who envisioned it as a decentralized monetary system that can effectively empower individuals and organizations in generating their own money.

Basically, Ripple is represented as debt. The transactions are simply composed of balances being transformed on a series of digital cash reserves from one user to another. Let us consider a simple example to explain how Ripple works in practice.

As a matter of fact, Ripple uses exactly the same specifications as Bitcoins aside from the primary byte in the address format. Hence, anyone can use the same keys to verify transactions and messages in the Ripple and Bitcoin networks. But instead of mining, the transactions in Ripple are basically propagated via the network, and a given set of contradictory transactions. For instance, let's say that a fraudulent user initiating transactions to send the same $50 to five various merchants with the hope of receiving $250 worth of goods. The clients should verify first which one received the payment first, and if unverified will be marked as illegitimate, via a process called consensus.

Other digital currencies that you might be interested to learn about are Dash, Manero, Altcoins, and many more.

CONCLUSION

Thanks again for taking the time to read this book!

After reading this book, I hope that you've gained ample knowledge about cryptocurrencies to be able to find enough confidence to get started. Just make sure that you do not act hastily as you are still participating in a monetary market.

In this case, it is important that you take your time, practice, and of course, have fun.

If you enjoyed this book, please consider taking the time to leave a review on the platform. Reviews are one of the easiest ways of supporting self-published authors!

www.ingramcontent.com/pod-product-compliance
Lightning Source LLC
Chambersburg PA
CBHW070314230526
45470CB00002B/867